ENTERING HISTORY

ALSO BY MARY STEWART HAMMOND

Out of Canaan

ENTERING HISTORY

POEMS

MARY STEWART HAMMOND

W. W. NORTON & COMPANY

Independent Publishers Since 1923

New York | London

Copyright © 2016 by Mary Stewart Hammond

For information about permission to reproduce selections from this book,
write to Permissions, W. W. Norton & Company, Inc.,
500 Fifth Avenue, New York, NY 10110

For information about special discounts for bulk purchases,
please contact W. W. Norton Special Sales
at specialsales@wwnorton.com or 800-233-4830

Manufacturing by RR Donnelley
Book design by JAM Design
Production manager: Lauren Abbate

Library of Congress Cataloging-in-Publication Data

Names: Hammond, Mary Stewart, author.
Title: Entering history : poems / Mary Stewart Hammond.
Description: First edition. | New York : W. W. Norton & Company, [2016]
Identifiers: LCCN 2016019247 | ISBN 9780393253962 (hardcover)
Classification: LCC PS3558.A453 A6 2016 | DDC 811/.54—dc23 LC record available at
https://lccn.loc.gov/2016019247

W. W. Norton & Company, Inc.
500 Fifth Avenue, New York, N.Y. 10110
www.wwnorton.com

W. W. Norton & Company Ltd.
15 Carlisle Street, London W1D 3BS

1 2 3 4 5 6 7 8 9 0

For Arthur forever

ACKNOWLEDGMENTS

Grateful acknowledgment to the editors of the following publications, in which these poems, sometimes in different forms, originally appeared, or are forthcoming:

Alaska Quarterly Review: "Days End on Eel Pond," "Heaven"

Barrow Street: "The Magic Dragon Missing His Mate," "Tapping Survival," "Born Again"

Persea Books: "Listening to the Radio"; also anthologized in *Where Books Fall Open*

Ploughshares: "Facing Eternity," "Portrait of My Husband Reading Henry James"

Shenandoah: "High Ground"; also anthologized in the textbook *Poetry: An Introduction*, Seventh Edition

The Kenyon Review: "Starting Over After Long Estrangement"

The New Criterion: "Reading the Declaration of Independence on the 4th of July," "The GWB in the Rain"; also anthologized in *Stone and Steel* and *The KGB Bar Book of Poems*

The New York Times Book Review: "The Art of Passing for Them"

The New Yorker: "Anniversary," "The Big Fish Story"; also anthologized in the textbook *The Bedford Introduction to Literature*, Tenth Edition

The Southern Review: "Entering History"

The Southwest Review: "Love & Marriage," "Jacob and Esau with Sister"

The Vineyard Gazette: "Seeing Mozart's Piano Quartet in E-flat Major in the Old Whaling Church, Edgartown"; also anthologized in *The Music Lover's Poetry Anthology*

The Yale Review: "LINES composed at Beaufort, South Carolina, a few miles above Parris Island," "Venasque"

My thanks also to Yaddo for giving me space and time where some of these poems could begin, or be completed.

CONTENTS

IV

V

VI

ENTERING HISTORY

I

ENTERING HISTORY

The door to the poem opens in, and a couple enter,
set down their luggage, and stand, backs to the door,
silhouetted against the light, taking in the room.

They step through French doors in the far wall and out
onto a balcony cantilevered over ramparts. The vast
impastoed Umbrian kingdom swoops away and down

before them. They have climbed this world in first
and second gear, half the afternoon, past twelfth-century belfries
and 500-year-old cypresses, up the very blacktop

switchbacking through the view. Dirt roads lead off it
wandering Etruscan boundaries to invisible purpose.
An ancient farm truck, no bigger than a pencil eraser,

and the only sign of life and the twenty-first century, crawls
soundlessly along one of them. On distant hills,
the honey and terra cotta of Assisi, Spello, Spoleto,

hover in the haze like cities of God fallen to earth,
habitations for humans the size of seeds
on white-haired dandelions. She leans her head on his shoulder.

———

He kisses her. They've already shrunk half an inch
since they began their lives together. They turn,
reenter the room, cross back and forth in profile, unpacking.

He's acquired a stomach, and his hair has gone white.
She pulls off her clothes. There is a scar on her breast,
one in her armpit; three more run like roads

across and down her belly. A bloom of spider veins
tattoos her calf. They're getting old, but not so old
we shouldn't close the door on their nap.

Tonight they'll have dinner downstairs.
Tomorrow they'll drive off into the view. For now,
they'll awaken in this minor city of God

entwined in each other's arms. We'll hear them talking,
sotto voce on the other side of the poem,
dusk erasing their bodies.

VACATION

When we travel we carry our baggage right out there
where we can see it, lock it, check it, hand-launder
its contents. It gives us the feel of baggage
as controllable, self-limited, a condition
with clear parameters. The rule of thumb is
boil things down to the essential,
that which you can easily push around.
When you think you have it to the minimum,
open your suitcase and remove two things.
That's right, the neurotic baggage has to go,
neurotic baggage being all that exceeds
two pairs of slacks, three shirts and a change of
    underwear,
which does not mean there won't be some
neurotic baggage left, curled up in a ball,
in the corners of your suitcase sucking its thumb, just that
that which can't fit into a wheelie and probably needs
treatment or drugs, gets a vacation from us, and that
that prayer of ours, the one that goes
Lord, give me no more than I can carry,
goes answered for a couple of weeks.

PORTRAIT OF MY HUSBAND
READING HENRY JAMES

Rather, it is in the shorter history of America,
not England, not Italy, that we find ourselves
in the perfect middle of a rainy, summer afternoon
inside a 1930s shingled boathouse long since
beached on a low hill out of water's reach,
and plumbed and electrified for habitation.
No effort has been made to hide its origins.
Old masts and spars wait in the overhead rafters.
Blocks and tackle, coiled in figure eight knots,
loop from hooks on the wooden walls' open studs.
The faded blue transom of Will-o'-the-Wisp,
my mother-in-law's 1920s childhood Sneakbox,
hangs on its traveler over the west window as if
the bow and midship had sailed off into the dark wood.

The person concerned sprawls in a Bean shirt
and Top-Siders in an easy chair by a slow fire
crackling like balled-up paper uncrumpling,
the length of him spilling on and on out over the ottoman.
He is meeting Isabel Archer, Madame Merle
and Gilbert Osmond while Duke Ellington's smooth
rationalizations slide out of speakers in a tease
of intrigues and blue notes played behind the beat,
major chords changing to minor, piano and sax

entwining. The face of our reader, caught in the fiction,
softens. The corners of his mouth turn up
just so. His hand rests on the top of his head.
His hair is silver. Ellington segues to Scott Joplin
to Bernstein. Firelight collects on his glasses.

He is in the pleasure of fine distinctions and
complicating clauses that match his own parsing of matters.
I want to stroke his cheek, but hesitate to break the spell.
He is both far away, and close enough to heave to
with, "Listen to this!" and "Ohhh. But this!"
and reads paragraphs, whole sections aloud
before he's off again. Or, he fetches up somewhere
in the middle distance wondering at "all these
oversexed characters!" (He reads little new fiction.)
As if in answer, *Rhapsody in Blue* rises up out of the clarinet
crying. But he's back in Rome beside the crinkling fire,
jazz working the room, shingles muffling the rain,
the sounds of a summer afternoon composing themselves
like time and happenstance entering and rippling in a human.

DAY'S END ON EEL POND

Sunlight spills through holes in the clouds
spotlighting the marsh grass here and not there,
whitening a sail out on the water, leaving
others in shadow, shining the transom
of the moored catboat, its bow disappearing.
The bobwhite calls its name without knowing it.

Sparrows and swallows, fussing and twittering
line up like deacons on the deck railing,
scooting off as one at some mysterious bidding.
The osprey's mousy squeak disguises
its six-foot wingspan, its preying nature.
Wind, rustling in the leaves of the choke cherry,

makes low whistles through the cedars
as it picks up, drops. Songbirds crowd
the air, zipping across the foreground
from candle pine to spruce to cedar.
In the distance the town clock strikes eight.
Somewhere a halyard chimes on a mast.

White, webbed chairs on the gray deck,
sit facing out, empty. At the deck corners,
white planters bristle with rosy orange geraniums.
The sun blazes in one window across the pond

as the others, two and three at a time, fill
with artificial light. A gull catches

a current, hangs suspended in it, screeches
like rusty hinges on a screen door,
and takes one last nosedive. The inlet sneaks
through beach grass and sand into the wide water,
and the sky beyond. Dusk softens the colors,
the geraniums' orange tang hanging on until dark.

VENASQUE

He'd build a fire, and bring me
strong, dark, bitter coffee every morning
with lots of milk, warmed, little sugar, just the way I like it,
and we'd sit opposite each other clutching our mugs
in a little loaned stone house in a little stone *village perché*
in Provence, in December, in the year 1991.

We probably said a few words.
Words of endearment. But we were each in a place
the other couldn't reach, and the winter landscape outside matched,
which is why we didn't want to look at it, had no room
to take it in because it was
already inside us.

What possessed us?
How could we forget Provence was on the same latitude as Nova Scotia?

He had brought a 1007-page book with him,
Robert Massie's *Dreadnought: Britain, Germany, and the Coming
of the Great War*, to be exact, although
that's less important than the number of pages.
It would be about here, after a few words, a few
swallows of coffee, when he would begin to read.
I had brought a blank notebook, but was frightened
of what I'd find there. I would begin to cry,

silently. Or, maybe it was the other way around;
I'd begin to cry, and then he'd pick up his book.
It doesn't matter. He was not shutting me out;
he was abandoning himself. He is a man who needs
certainty the way the rest of us need food, or sleep,
and he no longer had a perfect wife; he had a wife
who had just been treated for cancer, who
most certainly was going to live,
but might not.

He also learned,
the day before we flew to France, the way lovers do
in Disease of the Week movies, to frolic in lavender
and sunbeams, when facing death,
that he might not have a job when we got back.
And he was fifty-five years old.
That was possibly scarier than having a wife with cancer.

Excuse me, a wife who's "gotten over" cancer.
It is advisable when dealing with this disease
to think of it as being something like
first cousin, seventeen times removed, from a flu bug, because
language, after all is said and everything
possible done, is the only hot oil left to pour down
on the marauding cells of any second wave trying
to climb the ramparts. The second attempt to invade
has been known to succeed.
We, being everyone, don't talk about that.

That is the value of language.

On the other hand, language is quite
handy for getting cancer off the table when there are other issues like:
being jobless in America in 1991 at the age of fifty-five.
Which you can't treat at Christmastime sitting in Provence.
Actually, unemployment is a condition
that can be treated with language, but the odds of it being a cure
rank with the odds that fruits and vegetables will cure cancer.
Take spin, for example: Spin is extremely useful
once you've decided on a treatment of choice for staying alive
financially, or corporeally. After that it is probably better to look
straight ahead, turn neither to your right nor your left,
neither to positive or negative.

Everyone who survives treatment is said to have survived cancer.
The word "recovering" would be closer to reality, but instead
we have the hocus-pocus expression "cancer survivor." I am
"a cancer survivor." Hello. My name is Mary Stewart, no hyphen,
and I am "a cancer survivor."
(Notice. I use quotations marks.
Spin doctors do not.)
This is the opposite of an AA meeting. This is a lie. Or not a lie.
This is medicaleaze. The truth is
the only way you know you've survived cancer is when
you die of something else, meaning
you never know.

———

So he was pissed. At me.

Of course, it's dumb. But understandable.

At the bank for giving him notice.

At himself. Beyond idiocy. Beyond a woman's comprehension.

I could tear my hair out on that one.

He was by my side like his life depended on it no more.

He had been my shepherd through the valley from suspicion to biopsy
to diagnosis to surgery, through meticulous notes on treatment options,
four different opinions, none of which agreed. We get to choose,
eeny, meeny, miny, moe.

The question never answered? "What would your wife do?"

This is what the movies don't tell you about having, or not having, cancer,
and about having, or not having, employment:

1) You are all alone with this. It's just you
   and the shelter of whatever language you can muster.

2) That you are your own *village perché* clinging to the edge of a cliff
   where you can do nothing for each other.

3) Even friends have no access, unless they already have a passport
   stamped *village perché*. The rest, who understand where you are,
   don't like it any better than you do. It could happen to them.

4) You are walled up, sealed off. Only the enemy can get in.

5) You will have found powerlessness.

———

We didn't go out much. The road in and out of the village
was narrow, winding and steep. Dangerous,
it seemed to us, and we were already in enough danger. Besides,
everything was *fermé*, including the landscape,
like the last scene in *On the Beach* about the end of life.
The Bomb drops, wind spreads radiation over the globe
until it reaches Australia, and the cast dies in Rembrandt lighting.
No lavender. Nothing green and living. Dead leaves cling to grapevines.
Wind machines move them. Accurately. The moves are stubby.
A sheet of old newspaper rattles, miked, down an empty street.

Of course, in our scene, whatever goes on underneath the earth in winter
was still going on, but it required more imagination than we had available
to re-vegetate the brown and umber boulders of the Luberon.
Even the sky was open only 5 to 6 hours a day.
Meanwhile the mistral operated 24 hours through us.

When we could
bring ourselves to climb
into our rental car, we went to see the other *villages perchés*,
and saw them as through slivers of daylight
the width of arrow slits in castle walls.
Mostly, we sat in the little stone house with the dark
scratching at the windows trying to get in.
Somewhere, in the castle keep, screams
emitted from the dungeons, although
we were absolutely still and silent inside our house.

———

Depending
on atmospheric conditions, sometimes Mahler
or Beethoven joined us, courtesy of *Radio Classique*.

He didn't want me to know he was scared for us.
Or, he didn't want himself to know. He wasn't talking.
Maybe he didn't know the word for "scared."
Maybe he didn't know how to pronounce the word,
didn't know the language of the *village perché* he had landed in.
Maybe the language
hadn't been invented yet for stiff-upper-lipped men without a job.

It seemed better not to let on I knew.

Maybe he didn't want me to know he was scared I would die.
Maybe he didn't want himself to know.

We had always slept, arms and legs entwined,
loving the feel of the flesh of the other. Now, we couldn't bear
the feel of the other. It was not a rebuff. It was as if
every nerve was on fire, as if touch would scorch us.

We slept in Venasque on our backs,
arms to our sides, eyes open to the dark
until sleep closed them. This is survivable. All that is needed
is to know what *village perché* the other is in, and why,
what the time zone is, then wait,
a tourist suspended.

FACING ETERNITY

Automobiles rout the Eternal City,
their exhaust like slow acid, peeling
the skin and cartilage off statues,
slipping the spirit from its moorings, as
a million times a day, humans stand,
backs pressed to the wall in the narrow streets
to let cars pass. One step, two, sometimes
maybe even a string of uninterrupted steps, then,
backs to the wall, they bide their time,
while two, three, four, even a string of cars
and motorbikes growl and whine and buzz and honk,
threading through parked cars and pedestrians.
Even automobiles are brought to a standstill
by automobiles—eighteen, twenty, abandoned
in random clots that barricade the streets.
Only humans able to climb like monkeys
from fender to hood to fender can pass,
their rage rising like the heat off baked metal
like the woman in Ferragamo heels and Armani
using feet and hands and bum to clamber
over one such tangle, fuming in Italian, "In no
other country in the world. . . !" But mostly,
humans stand quietly, our backs to the wall,
our backs to the wall, our backs to the wall,
acting out the place we've come to.

LOVE & MARRIAGE

It is beyond me, how, after all these years, you
can still get so heated up when I'm
not ready on time. Some things

should be taken for granted, like
the banging on the car roof that begins
one block from home of the suitcase you

forgot to put in the trunk because I
wasn't ready on time, or like the dignified
snap of *The New York Times* I open,

like a Berlin wall, between us
(and, *bien sûr*, my tongue is stuck out behind it),
so I won't see you take the wrong cloverleaf that

always awaits us, no matter what I say, rarely
more than a few miles into any trip,
the one that has us, this time, hurtling

east instead of west. One hour later
I've finished the paper and you're surprised
it's Philadelphia we're approaching, not

———

Altoona, which is, of course, due to my
not being ready on time, which means, now,
we're foaming-at-the-mouth late and I-295 is just

"driving" you, "without mercy," into the heart of downtown,
which you tell me to get you out of because I
got you into it. I offer the teensiest "uhhmmm," nothing

the least bit inflammatory—*au fond,*
inflammatory is hardly necessary—and spittle
flies from the corners of your mouth. All by yourself

you handle the City of Brotherly Love with shouts of "Bugger,"
which you seem to think is more genteel than "Fuck."
Inner-city Philly cowers before the Anglo-Saxon.

Eventually, even King of Prussia steps aside
and lets you pass. Two hours into the trip
and we're finally on our way. I do love

the moral high ground, and cover it with chirping
commentary on the passing countryside you say
you can't see because you can't

take your eyes off the road because
you're driving so fast because
I wasn't ready on time. You make me read

———

the business report you are to give. Every word.
We're off the Turnpike and entering the hills
when I finish. I offer the peace of an idea.

You tell me it's already been done.
I haven't even told you what it is.
The road narrows. We drop into second gear.

The moral high ground is beginning to seem a lot
like the Appalachian soil outside our windshield—
not all that rewarding—and the scent of woodsmoke

wafts through the car windows. It carries me
back to the mountains of Virginia, to my people,
my roots. It returns me to those early days of conflict resolution,

before Freud, ahead of the sheriff, or the preacher.
I'm up to my eyeballs in the sun-baked crusts of horse manure,
the cow pies and warm chicken droppings you've dumped

on the passenger side of the car, and I feel a wad of something
like chewing tobacco form between my lip and gums.
My mouth waters with words. My mouth runneth over

with words. I take aim. Yea, though I hock a brown juice
stream of words straight in your direction, I speak no evil,
only truth, five minutes of full-volume truth, segueing

———

into every evil man ever did to woman.

Mopping your brow, you say, "Now, what brought that on?"

And I say, "Love, honey. Love and marriage."

THE BIG FISH STORY

Late fall. Not a soul around for miles.
Just me and my man. And those scallopers
trolling a few hundred feet offshore I'm pointing to,
emphatically, saying No, Non, Nein, Nyet, Nej,
in every language, including Body English,
in response to his idea that we take off
all our clothes smack in the middle of the lawn
in broad daylight and go swimming!
This is the line he throws me: "But, sweetheart,
the young have given up scalloping.
Those are all old men out there.
Their eyesight is terrible." Which explains why
I'm naked in the water off the coast
of Massachusetts on the 14th of October
and loving it, the water still summer warm
feeling like silk, like the feel of his flesh
drawing over my skin when we're landed
on a bed, so I swim off out of his reach
lolling and rolling, diving and surfacing,
floating on my back for his still good eyes.
I know what he has in mind and what
I have in mind is to play him for a while
for that line I swallowed, delay the moment
I'll do a slow crawl over to him,
wrap my legs around his waist, and
reel him in—just the fish he was after.

II

LINES

composed at Beaufort, South Carolina,
a few miles above Parris Island

Five days have passed; five days with the length
of five long nights, and nothing has changed,
not I, not my brother's mind, not the world's.
It takes ten days, the duty sergeant said,
for discharge papers, and I unpacked, and waited.
Mornings, I sketch boats nodding on the sun.
Nights, I study a rare collection of antebellum mansions
drawling around a quiet port with the musky smell
of Hepplewhite and Adam on their breath. Afternoons,
I spend at the Base Dispensary, waiting to see my brother,
driving the eight-mile hyphen between morning and night
cocooned in the car radio's full-volume bravado.
At the sentry box I present my Visitor Pass,
reserved for families of graduates, the injured,
the suicidal.

Inside the Island's barbered tropics,
crew-cut grass, and topped palm trees hung
with hanks of untamed Spanish moss, muster
in precision through azaleas and birds of paradise.
Signs coming and going on the roadways boast
WE TRAIN THE WORLD'S BEST KILLERS, and platoons,
fresh from bayoneting sandbag bodies, scoring

hits on pop-up, plywood humans, drill and stomp
to breakfast, lunch and dinner shouting
Oh yeah, Oh yeah, ready to fight, ready
to die, ready to kill with all our will!
Oh yeah, Oh yeah. . . .

            And I retreat to Beaufort and talk to ghosts,
drawing comfort from Federal and Greek Revival dwellings,
water-turned, catching breezes under discreetly-raised,
white-columned porches, each a temple to love
because Miss Judith (shall we call her),
slept six months with Sherman to save her town
from burning, or just because. In any case,
the town was saved, to its everlasting shame.
It endures, a tribute to the act of love,
without honor, and curves around the bay
like dirty linen for all the world to wonder
why it is the only town left untouched in all the path
of Sherman's holocaustic march.

                    And, Miss Judith?
Was she the fairest and purest? Or, maybe
a young widow of three years and four months?
Could the town do nothing to stop the collaboration,
or did it not want to? Where is honor in a place
captured and occupied? Consider the consequences:
She climbed into Sherman's bed, he didn't torch the place,
she was shunned, and the town became sire and heir of its shame.

When Sherman withdrew, he left plugged in his place, a dildo
of memory, each spared house, a mark of collaboration,
a tabby A on its chest, sealing the town in a borrowed time.
Such a nice girl, the whisper runs down to this day.
*From one of our finest families, too. And he was
no gentleman!*

> *Ah, General. Cump, I understand
> they call you—if I may be so familiar—for Tecumseh. A coup,
> a stroke of genius hoisting them on your blade, dangling
> with the thought they honored you by their mere existence.
> Your face is saved in theirs, and their face,
> unbaptized by the cleansing fire, is ruined.
> How you must have loved looking back as you
> and your army rode away, seeing your manhood risen
> tattletale white and glistening in the sun—not just one,
> but ten, twenty, forty houses with your seed
> pulsing through their halls and English basements,
> joining you to them, for so long as they shall stand.
> What more could any man want? Did you know
> fire would make them victims, that survival would destroy
> their face more than fire, would leave them sipping bourbon
> on upstairs wooden porches staring off to sea
> for generations, rocking tangled feelings
> in complaining wicker chairs, dwelling endlessly
> in their dwelling in their dwelling*

Or do I wrong him? Was the town

his parting gift to Judith, given out of love? He did
like giving towns as gifts; Savannah's destruction
he called his "Christmas gift" to Lincoln. The destruction
of other towns, he called "gifts" to General Grant.
Or were the houses, turned into hospitals, spared
because they still held the Union wounded. *What was it Cump?*
Tell me it was love. Tell me it was a touch of the man
peering through the soldier. And to her I whisper,
What made you do it? Why, when he lay in your arms,
gentled, legs weakened, unmanned, didn't you
behead him? There she is, in the shadows, looking at me
amused. Oh, but then she's gone. *Don't leave!*
I need to know. But what does it matter?
The North and the South lay down together, enemy
with enemy, with the whole town desiring it,
feeling themselves traitors because of their desire
and, when the two sides rose, the town still stood.

          Now, its peccant splendor harbors me,
gives me sanctuary against my anxious days.
It nourishes, feeds, and houses me, this town
twice occupied. Not alone the Union Army,
but now by Marines from the Base, who traffic
like unowned ghosts through the wall of preoccupation.
The town's conditioned left-hand, once again,
money-changes war into room and board, and that
little extra, a coat of paint, new front steps,
even a little AT&T. Compromise is still

their grits and bourbon, and the spared houses
cast flat, oblong shadows like coffin lids
over bumpy brick sidewalks. I step from one
to the other, watching the proud headlights
and taillights passing on the distant bridge
for the daily Boot Camp graduations, and lean my cheek
against a tabby house to touch the rough sides of love,
finding comfort in its lastingness.

                                        Eight miles away,
prepared for battle, my broken brother, ready to die
with all his will, but not to kill, shoelaceless, marches
his shaven head and beltless green fatigues into insanity.
Our preacher father blames himself for coupling
God's word to his own commands of "Obey!"
delivered at the end of a belt, and wonders
if his son is weak,
      and the song we learned in Sunday school
            Jesus loves the little children,
      runs in my head,
            all the children of the world
      or is he strong?
            red and yellow, black and white
      And the preacher is down on his knees
            they are precious in His sight,
      on a sandy beach near Parris Island
            Jesus loves
      weeping, praying for words, his palms clutching

        the little children
    each other, begging the unanswerable God,
        of the world.
    "What do I say to my son, now?"

The wait time to see my brother is long, and the visits
short: ten minutes. He is brought, marching,
from his cell to the Visitor's Room. He does not
embrace me when he sees me. He doesn't see me.
He is marching. In circles. Punching the air with one arm,
shouting the Marine Corps chant, holding up his pants
with the other. But sometimes he stops,
falls in my arms, but not for long,
and I croon to him in tongues, this split son
of our world's creation, stroke the stubble
on the face he buries in my lap, and then he's up
and marching again.

                    At dusk I drive back
to Beaufort where the windows of the houses
curving around the gulf glow like a necklace
on Judith's throat. Oh, dear Father, judge not,
judge not. This is all we have for answers:
Your son can't hear us. His voice is almost gone.
Yet, still he raves his manhood into padded walls,
marching our questions onward off to war,
around and around Cell Block 4, rasping

Oh yeah, Oh yeah, ready to fight, ready to die,
ready to kill with all my will, Oh yeah. . . .
the tears he doesn't cry running
these five days along my cheeks.

ON THE USES OF PAPER FOR LOCATING
AND DISCHARGING GUILT

Eyes, open like the dead, rise out of the AP photo
from the faces of five- and six-year-olds
cowering in a freshly dug ditch, and stare down

the green pastures of Sunday readers
settled in with their second cup, seeking
averted hearts for a resting place;

for the record, the ditch is as good as
nursery school: for milk and cookies they have
the unquestionable security of an M16

cradled in the arms of an American soldier who is,
according to the picture's caption, "protecting
children from enemy sniper bullets,"

while the sounds of machine gun fire
stand their childhood up against the wall
of grown-ups, perforating it into good copy,

paper children captured in newsprint to be recycled
Sunday night, nothing more than a chunk of headline,
the corner of an ad where flesh and face might be,

———

or ripped off along the perforations,
clipped and filed away like payment stubs,
like a debt paid, like

like little well-wrought conceits,
exploited as balm for the conscience
of journalist and poet.

STARTING OVER
AFTER LONG ESTRANGEMENT

To all appearances they are having dinner,
the two women sitting halfway back
along the left wall of the Caffe Grazie.

They've come from the Met museum where
they wandered side by side, as they used to years ago,
talking diagonals, frontal planes, brushwork.

A sudden downpour has driven them here.
Now they are face-to-face. They raise their glasses,
laugh nervously, clink, sip, dip bread in olive oil,

focus on the menu, talk lobster and coriander reduction,
the earthiness of cauliflower custard. Light
from votive candles wavers over them.

The past is not mentioned. It has been declared
off limits. It is not clear by which one,
but it sits between them, a black hole, its

gravitational field waiting to suck them in.
But it won't. They are here "getting on with their lives,"
"without the baggage of the past," without amends,

———

talking *salade composé*, talking pumpkin polenta, talking
potato gnocchi. Rain blinds the Caffe's street front window,
like tears behind contact lenses. These two are not

having dinner. They are reaching their arms
out across the unbridgeable abyss,
dancing from foot to foot on its rim, crying

"Mamma! Mamma!"
"My daughter! My daughter!"
talking *granité aux fraises*, talking espresso.

Or maybe only one of them is calling.

SEEING MOZART'S PIANO QUARTET IN E-FLAT MAJOR IN THE OLD WHALING CHURCH, EDGARTOWN

They wait, five women in black,
before a wall painted such a flat, soft gray
it reads as silence, or sky.
The pianist's hands curve over the keyboard.
The page turner leans toward the pianist's score.
The violinist, the violist, the cellist
bring their bows near the strings. Fluted pilasters
rise into an arch, ceiling high, framing them.
The church, classic Greek Revival
straight from the style books, and *retardataire* at that,
is fifty-seven years younger than the music that is about
to be played, but with its pillars, its two
center aisles dividing the nave into three parts,
in its classicism and its purity, it is useful
for showing the architecture of this sonata.
The thing about music, it takes place in time,
and can't be seen. Nor can it be reproduced in a poem.

A colorless, unfinished, eight o'clock sky pauses
in triple hung windows flanking the pilasters.
Scrub oak darken the lower panes.
The pianist nods.
We know from the musicians' movements
that Mozart's allegro begins its lift

off the pages on the music stands, but here
there are only words, as black and white
as a picture show before the arrival of sound.
The pianist misses some notes.
The violist looks at the violinist,
her hair a stubble three months after chemo.
Strings shine on the black necks of the instruments.
The musicians' fingers climb up and down like spiders,
thumbs hugging the backsides of the necks.
They glide their bows, or make them tiptoe,
forearms rigid, across the strings.

The second theme's leading motif, almost lost
under the angelic, repeats and repeats
like supplications. It is one of Mozart's miracles,
this longing under joy, the flirtations with death
balancing lyricism. The ensemble coaxes the allegretto
and transubstantiation from wooden boxes. In a year
the violist will be dead,
but for now she plays Mozart. The music breathes
in the musicians' bodies. You can see it
in their shoulders, their spines, their wrists, their fingers,
and the white grid of the windows' muntins cages the black sky.
Even where the bottom sashes open to the summer air,
the night is held back until the musicians stop,
hold their poses, wait, five seconds, twelve,
for the last notes to find home, and fling up their arms
pumped with arrival. They rise, bowing
before the firmament of the soft gray wall.
The lights come up in a country church.

ANNIVERSARY

July 31, 1965

Tonight they were bringing my brother up from the deep,
nothing so grand as the sea, merely
a quarry in Georgia, barely
a mile or two wide and flooded
to a depth of 200 feet, no bigger
in the scheme of things
than a soup spoon's bowl,
but it held him, it cradled him,
this place vast as death,
small as life. It reduced him
to a speck in the universe.
The size of him, after all,
was vast and small.
It filled the spoon; it disappeared.

III

THE ART OF PASSING FOR THEM

Please. Get back in your body. All I said was
"I'm a poet." I tried not to. We get along fine
until then, talking about golf which I don't play,
and tennis which my friends pay me
not to play, about how much you hate teachers
because they ruined your life, left you hating
everything, so all you can do is "make money,
and know nothing. Nothing! Horrible people, teachers.
Horrible! I hope you don't know one,"
and since I am one, I know I'm passing.
It must be the pearls. The off-the-shoulder dress.

Tonight, for you and me, the setting is a Gala,
and for charity's sake we're seated together,
except you're paying cash, and I'm "comped,"
a prop for the evening, asked to fill a table and pass
for an Angel, Benefactor, Patron among the real donors,
so they will think my kind is their kind, or
the kind of kind they want to associate with, and thus
will donate money to whatever the cause
which, in this case, is the cause of literature.
After golf, tennis, your academic career,
your wine cellar, your favorite ski slopes,
your new, improved, costly wife and gifted children,
it comes to you to ask what I do.

I know where this is going.
This is going to where the poem began, so I go,

"Well, I used to shoot clay pigeons," and I learn
all about the best gauge shotgun, and the merits
of side by side vs. over and under, for killing birds.
This can get us through the entrée. Sometimes,
it doesn't. Sometimes, we run out of discussable guns, so
you ask what I do when I'm not at the shooting range.
Like a politician, I don't answer the question.
I ask about bailouts. This gets you going
on free market *laissez-faire*, about which
I have an opinion, but keep to myself since
I'm here to pass as one of you. "But what,"
you ask, "do you do, now?" Actually,
women over forty are rarely asked this question
by men. They know what we do. We do
our hair, lunch, our nails. We shop. They think.

(*Double entendre*, that.) Yes, I'm stereotyping you,
but now I'm the one with the pen, the computer,
writing history in an off-the-shoulder dress.
Politesse says, soon, I should turn to the man on my left,
who is playing with his device under the tablecloth
(which, to give him the benefit of the doubt, I assume
is electronic), so I can hear about his golf game,
his backhand (we'll leave mine out of this),
his wine cellar, and not have to see you, man

on my right, leave your body, as everyone does,
when I answer the "what do you do" question.

I hate when that happens. It makes me feel disappeared,
but you are really trying to hold up your end of things, so,
instead of turning to my left, I mutter, "I'm a writer."
Those with acute hearing recognize in that
a polite follow-up question. "What kind of writer?"
A good one, is the answer that comes to mind. Instead,
I sit up straight and say, "Well. I used to be a journalist,"
as if being a journalist makes it okay to be a poet.
What I want to say is think of me as a bond trader.
There's nothing special about being a poet.
We plod along making words syllable by syllable,
like you make money derivative by derivative,

and we're no smarter than you, and no more suicidal
than your plumber. Some of us aren't even weird,
although it is weird to want to do something that isn't
going to make any money, and has no chance
of being optioned for a movie, and, believe me, this
scares poets more than it scares you. "A journalist?"
You're looking very interested at this point.
"What kind of journalist?" "A sportswriter, actually."
And the whole world of football, boxing, hockey,
baseball opens up, and we arrive at dessert without me
ever having to say "Poet." Except, since this is a Gala,
the end of the meal marks the beginning of the program,

and I have yet to turn to the man on my left, as protocol
requires, who is still fiddling with his device,
to the dismay of the woman on his left.

First off, people have to be thanked and applauded.
Many people. Many, many, many. This can take
a very long time, adding to the suspense of when, if ever
the big box office After Dinner Speaker will speak.
Tonight it's a famous poet introducing another famous poet,
bestowing on us an exegesis of the honoree's full
oeuvre, leaving three minutes for the honoree
to read from his oeuvre. (This is not yet a recognized
competitive sport.) It's pearls before a black tie crowd
sated with food and wine who don't like poetry.
They support the disabled, musicians, stray dogs, poets.
They just don't want to have to sit next to one.

Forty minutes into the intro, you whisper in my ear,
"You'll be happy to know, he only has twenty pages to go."
A bonding moment! Then, comes the Decaf moment.
This is when you say, "What kind of sportswriter?"
I dread answering this almost as much as I dread
saying "Poet." "Yacht racing?" I make it a question
knowing it sounds effete, not like a real sport to anyone
who has never covered yacht races on 50' boats
in the middle of the Atlantic in gale force winds
with 30' following seas, and seven men.
It's the second most dangerous sport of all.

I explain this so when we get to the start of the poem,
when I say I'm a poet, you'll know I'm not a girlie poet.
I'm not a macho poet, either, like those guys
who write about food and babies when girls can't;
it labels you minor if you're a girl, but not if you're a guy.
Poets are just regular, normal, neurotic human beings,
who, according to the latest survey, are even more stable
than fiction writers, yet everybody loves to sit
next to fiction writers. They could have a best-seller
in their laptops, meaning money, and money means
some way of valuing what they do sitting home alone all day.

"Are you still doing that, covering yacht races?"
"No, I do something more dangerous." "What's that?"
"I'm a poet." There I've said it. And there you have it.
The poem's whole *apologia pro vita sua*—you
with your eyes emptying, me left sitting next to your suit.
I tug on its sleeve. Please, get back in your body. At least,
talk to the pearls, the off-the-shoulder dress.

A POEM FOR OLDER PEOPLE

A non-Twitterer wanted to know what FB meant?
That was me, actually.
Next, I needed to know what BF meant.
Someone older, a hedge funder, wanted to know what xo meant.
I explained xo means hugs and kisses, but is noncommittal.
It's more than "Best regards," closer to "Warm regards"
without getting personal. It's like I kinda like you,
but not much. Don't use it in a business letter. Ever.
Yes, no matter how much you like your cubicle mate, or boss.
All it means is you're okay in my book, and nothing more.
xoxo is a deeper commitment. It means Fondly,
without the stiffness of signing "Fondly."
xoxoxo means Really Fond of You, which can't be
written out because it sounds, I mean, like creepy.
xoxoxxoxxx is close to "Love," without being love,
and LOL is not what you think it is.
Of course, "Love" now suffers from emotion inflation,
thrown around like an A– on high school report cards.
but it feels good. It's the distance between the "I adore you"
of the old days, and "I love you," which was a really
deep commitment, one step removed from Will you marry me?
But that was then. Now it has nothing to do with marriage.
Now, it isn't even a necessary metaphor for Can I get into your pants?

———

This gets us to "Cheers," or it doesn't, but we need to talk about it.
It is an issue. The first time I ever saw "Cheers"
as the closing of a letter, was on a Christmas card from JC,
not that JC, but he was someone we all thought
walked on water. Being self-involved, I took it personally.
It was an OMG moment. (We all know what that means.)
I took it to mean JC applauds me, admires me, congratulates me,
tips his hat to me. If you are self-involved, it doesn't matter for what.
I was in a swoon. You couldn't talk to me for days.
Not long after, "Cheers" went viral. JC must have sent
"Cheers" to everyone. Everyone was signing off "Cheers."
It was, you must admit, a contagious sign-off.
I no longer took it personally. Or used it.
It was so over. It wasn't even an upgrade of xo.

So where are we? We're here, and now you know.
And this is the end.

xo Mary Stewart (It's a double name, no hyphen.)

IV

JACOB AND ESAU WITH SISTER

Even before recorded history, Jacob lived.
When he wasn't threatening to sue, he dreamed.
In Hebrew, his name means heel grabber, leg puller
for trying to keep his twin brother, Esau, from emerging first
from the womb. He is also called, for good reason,
supplanter, deceiver, this son of Isaac gone blind,
grandson of Abraham, brother, in blood only, to Esau. Yet,
centuries later, it is he we see snoozing in oil paintings,
his head cushioned on a rock in the desert of his fathers.
See him in the same pose in Sunday School coloring books.
See him oil his way into your living room. You may know him.

Jacob dreams he is climbing the corporate ladder,
but he has never set foot inside a corporation.
He doesn't believe the entry rung is for him.
At the top of the ladder are chairmen of the board
who look a lot like angels, and know his worth.
They hold out to him a gold parachute for failing.

Where is Esau? He is working the fields, plowing, sowing,
reaping, hunting game, earning his keep from B.C. to A.D.
Now, thirty-six centuries old, he is long-hauling
copper and railroad ties, and Rebar in an 18-wheeler
from Hebron to Canaan, through Galilee to Appalachia.
It was a given he'd wind up a tired truck driver the day

he pulled into Genesis exhausted, famished, facing
bankruptcy, his jeans empty, and found his twin brother,

lying around quaffing the grape, acting like cock of the walk,
living off their father, Isaac, The Easily Duped, using
the Heimlich maneuver to make him cough up extra talents
of silver to support him, his wife, and children, to buy them
a new tent, new hardwood floors, a slate roof, another
business, to upgrade their camels to a Cadillac and Lexus.
After all, they were a deal, I mean, a deal. Of course, Jacob
does nothing in return, except he doesn't see it that way.

So, here's the situation. We have two brothers standing face to face
in the middle of Genesis. One is exhausted and starving.
That's Esau. The other is stirring a pot of lentils. That's Jacob.
They eye each other. They eye the bubbling pot.
You know the plot. Esau says, in his polite Southern way,
I'm mighty hungry. May I have some?
Jacob says, *Sure. Hand over your birthright.*
(Jacob, as we have seen, is skilled in this kind of deal.)
Esau sticks up his hands, and surrenders his inheritance.

Theologians have no problem with this. They blame Esau
for agreeing to such a trade. He lacked mojo, or he despised
his birthright, or was careless of it, or had not been properly
parented and felt himself worthless, or felt he had no right
to his birth, or didn't understand what he was signing.
The spoils, including the storytellers, go to the victor.

Thus, it is writ: If you're took, you're took.
A deal's a deal. This is the Old Testament.
And it's their story, and they're sticking to it.

What kept any author of that reimagined history from asking
Can none of us imagine the aroma of a pot of lentils
held like a gun to the nose of a man ready to die of hunger?
What is a birthright worth to such a man?
What kind of brother takes such advantage of a brother?
What kind of descendants are we not to question
what kind of brother asks for so much in return for so little?
What kind of brother doesn't just give a morsel from the pot
to a starving brother? Answer: A brother hungry for a kingdom,
with no collateral but a pot of lentils, a stew of failed
get-rich-quick schemes, and his father's blindness.
And this is the one featured in oil paintings?

In Jacob's dreams he is the prince of God, and his name
shall be Israel, and this name will be given him by God.
God will do this without wrestling with him to confess his sins.
He will become a leader of men rich in cattle, silver and gold.
He will stretch his pot of beans into a meal off others.
It is written in the stars. The cash register will ring.

When awake, he rails against Isaac, son of Abraham,
for his failures. He'd be rich and famous now, he rants,
a national success, if Isaac hadn't cut off the money stream
after fifty years. But worry not for Jacob.

He is writing a book about George Bush and Jesus.
It will make millions, not counting the movie rights.

Before the sand began to blind already blind Isaac's mind,
he saw Jacob had tricked him into blessing him, the wrong son,
the younger son, the smooth-skinned, hairless second son, kneeling
before him, his arms covered with animal skins, the better to fake
firstborn Esau's hairy arms, and his smell of the fields.
But Isaac didn't know how to undo his mistake
without getting Jacob pissed off, make him threaten again
to keep his grandchildren from him, so he stood by it.
None of it mattered anyway.

Jacob didn't need Esau to sign away his inheritance.
Jacob just helped himself to what was left of fields
and goats, understanding camels and dreams were not
the future. The future was his for the taking. It was simple really.
When Isaac died, all he needed to do was forge his signature,
put words in Isaac's mouth, and backdate the tablet.

Like so many stories of fathers and sons, the withholding son,
given so much, knew the power of withholding love, and left Isaac
to live in squalor, and Esau to live penniless in a trailer park.
What to do? What can anyone do now that it's done?

O sister, asleep on your bed of roses, missing
from Genesis, and all its subsequent books. Wake up!
Tell the truth. You weren't missing. You were on tiptoe

in the background, seeing and not seeing, not letting on,
even to yourself, any of this, blind as Isaac, until too late.
Isaac abandoned is where this story always ends. What's left
but to tell it? Then, go back to sleep. Go back to dreaming.
It runs in the family. Dream a little tenderness.

WELTS

Don't hit little children.
Their skin is like butter.

The welts don't fade.
They sink

into the soul. It is possible
to cut open the souls

of beaten children and count
the welts like growth rings,

evidence they carry with them
for the life of the soul,

longer than any other mark
you will leave on the planet.

FAMILY

Who better than I understand religion
as a cloak for rage? If the heart is masochistic,

experience teaches nothing. I avoid shortcuts
and parks after dark, yet persist in reasoning

with Bible-thumpers. And why not?
If I want to get fucked, who does it better than family?

Cozy up, and they cease being content
with their hands in my pockets. Take their words

out of my brain, and they have the excuse
they were looking for. The anger-dependent don't need

to cut to the quick. I'm a survivor. I'm lying back
enjoying it, doing as I'm told, to escape with my hide.

The day I stop enjoying it is the day that I die.
It is the day of estrangement, the day the mourning begins.

BORN AGAIN

Sometimes things are done to you
and when you finally come up
out of your hole

seasons later
you're not the fox you were
when you went to ground.

You are, maybe, the fox
you were meant to be
all along. Most certainly

the fox you are now
is the critter no one would ever
have done things to in the first place.

WATCHING THE SUN SET
IN THE EAST

The sun, no longer in the sky, but balancing
like a forgotten beach ball between two spruce
on the far western edge of the lawn,
throws a last shaft of light eastward,
two or three miles across Nantucket Sound,
illuminating Chappaquiddick's long orange bluff,
its gray-green nap of vegetation,
and the underside of gulls
flying into its slant, the rays
carried on their bellies as easy
as radioactivity.

V

HEAVEN

My plane slips the tarmac imperceptibly as the spirit
departing, and the shadow of the left wing follows aft
gliding over the lower world. There, in a hospital room

no bigger than the cell in a honeycomb, my mother
struggles to rise from her wheelchair. She must succeed
at this in order to go home. She believes

in the Resurrection of the body. The one she's in, but
newer. Her arms tremble from Parkinson's and effort.
Or from pain in the spine she fractured. Or from heart failure.

So far, she can raise herself only two inches.
Yesterday, while trying, she said she was ready
for her new body. My father claims she meant

she was ready to die. I claim she was joking. She meant
she could use that new body now, not in the hereafter.
When he leaves each night, they kiss goodbye as if parting

forever. In the morning, when he returns, and they see
they live, their soul kisses shut out the underworld.
Today, driving me back to the airport he said he would do

---

anything to have her home again. Anything. And far below,
inside one of the toy cars I see scurrying over the causeways
threading Tampa Bay, the speck of my father speeds

my mother's soiled laundry to the washer and dryer
at their earthly home. It's a long drive. It's something.
My plane turns north climbing into the future. There,

in Manhattan, not yet on the radar, my own love
strides from the market into the honeycomb of our apartment
preparing a lunch of bread and wine and cheese

to gather me in. And someday, he, too, will die.
The plane rocks so slightly it could be
hung from a bough, stopped dead

in kingdom come. The engine's hum
swaddles me. We've reached altitude.
I push the button in my armrest. My seat reclines.

In its pitch, I am bigger than life, godly, unreachable.
I don't want to return to the earth.
The windows are empty with clouds.

CADILLAC

So this is what it all comes to, this
shuffling behind a three-wheel walker.
Her Cadillac she calls it, trying to sound

witty and charming, but we know she names it
for the Cadillac her son bilked her out of,
that the joke hides sarcasm and the ache of betrayal,

he tooling around like a bandit with good suspension,
while she is left gripping the handlebars of a walker.
Clearly, that chapter of the story has not yet

vanished into the holes in her mind
where other pieces of her life reside.
Soon, that part, too, will be gone.

THE WAY IT GOES

She looks for her dead son, and
her past, and, hmmm, what? yes,

that's it, what she wants
for her future, up

where the wall meets
the ceiling,

the aluminum curtain track
out of mind, if not

out of sight, and past and future
climb the wall,

meet the ceiling.

THE MAGIC DRAGON MISSING HIS MATE

There was the way my father used to puff on his glasses
and polish them with a Kleenex. Then, the way

he put slices of Velveeta on shredded wheat biscuits
and toasted them in the oven for our Saturday breakfast.

And then, well, I can't remember.
An old black and white photo has been ripped in half,

vertically. All I see now is my father standing
in the middle distance, near the photo's torn edge,

his back to us, the light, stopped down,
flattening him to a silhouette, the way children

often see their parents, and walking away from us,
as is a parent's job, into the mountains of Virginia.

They are gray and blurry in the photo, and blend
into the sky at the top margin. You can tell he is walking

away. See the heel of one foot, the toe of the other,
positioned on the horizonless ground. See his right arm

———

held at a 30-degree angle away from his body. His hand is missing. It's in the torn-off part, out in the ether holding his mate's.

None of this is true. The photo doesn't exist. This is just the way it is.

GATE 35

My father is dying in FL. He is still breathing
in, breathing out. I'm still at LGA, breathing
in, breathing out. The flight is delayed.
1 hour. 2 hours. 6 hours. Breathe in,
breathe out. He is skin and bones, 6' of him down
to 5'4" and 129 lbs. breathing in, breathing out.

After 1 hour we are gathered like sheep at the Gate.
After 6 hours, we've become family, new friends.
They notice my altered breathing. They stroke my shoulder,
pat me, rub my back. Sympathy is the thing I can't handle.
It makes me cry. And I do.

The loudspeaker pages passengers, announcing
the next flight to FL, not ours, to Indianapolis,
Boston, West Palm, anyplace but Tampa/St. Pete.
We sit in wire chairs, on the floor, some asleep,
some reading, everyone breathing.

The next announcement comes to us from the ceiling.
The plane has a weight and balance problem.
Delta needs 6 volunteers to give up their seats.
Stop breathing. Will 6 people step forward in time?

_____

Is this what life is like, all of us waiting for departure?
My daughter says, "Relax. Your father isn't going anyplace."
Not true. He has already begun his ascension.

NO MORE

At 89, my father had a stroke. He regained the use of his left side,
but not his left hand. He couldn't crack an egg.
He couldn't both hold the phone and push its numbers.
Then, he was 90, and 91. Sometimes he tried to put both legs
into one leg of his trousers, wanted Velcro to close his shirts.

I kept a small bag packed by the front door, the way I did
when my due date was near, and I was ready to be delivered.
After his stroke, I was ready for the middle-of-the-night call,
the dash I would make to the hospital by way of LGA
to Tampa/St. Pete. The bag sat there. He turned 92, and 93.
He said he was tortured in his mind.

Each ring of the phone stopped my heart. Each, I was sure,
was the call to say my father was due to be delivered of his body.
Each was a junk call. Between, I made weeklong visits
requiring a big suitcase and a carry-on. Like a hamster,
I traveled nowhere but back and forth to Florida.
The terminal became the terminal hyphen connecting us.

He turned 94. At 94 and ½ the call wasn't junk.
I grabbed my small bag by the front door,
ready with its quart-size ziplock bag
packed with carefully measured 4-ounce toiletries,
a couple of changes of underwear, a nightgown,
the wrinkle-free black dress, and ran.

For the first time since, I'm back at LGA, back in our hyphen,
delivered of my other self. It's a partial birth.
The big suitcase is packed and checked
for another place. My carry-on rolls over the same
polished stone floor. I walk in yesterday's footsteps.
My eyes flood with tears. I liberate my boarding pass
from the kiosk, inch along the queue for security,
remove shoes and jacket, get scanned, retrieve
my personal effects, walk downhill to the gate,
down the Jetway, onto a plane, find my seat. Sit. Wait.
The plane taxis down the runway as if it were still June,
lifts off, turns north to Massachusetts.

AFTER LIFE, THIS

JetBlue goes from 0 to 150 in 30 seconds and lifts
from the murk into the sunshine where my father
wafts on the other side of the window
suspended in the upper, pure, bright air.

He is wearing street clothes, and a clerical collar.
He never wore one when he was below.
He considered them fig leaves, a flaunting of rank
before the flock. I am adorned, head to toe, in fig leaves.

He points this out to me, even now, through the window.
See the forefinger of his dead hand wagging.
See my gold earrings, my good cloth coat, my diamond ring.
See him struggle to remove his belt.

He wants me to know I am loved.
He mouths "Proverbs 13:24," as if I didn't remember
to spare the rod is to hate your children, and
oh, how we were loved.

Norman Rockwell magazine covers were his vision of our family.
He moves his arms as if swimming up from the deep.
He is trying to find heaven.
He is trying to find Mother.

She is hiding.

LAST WORD

When parents are on their deathbed,
we are told to say to them, even
if they are unconscious,
the final thing we need to say.

I would lie.
This is not the time for truth.

VI

READING THE DECLARATION OF
INDEPENDENCE ON THE 4TH OF JULY

for Rob

It is a tradition in this family, to gather after lunch on the 4th
under a pavilion built on the flat roof of an old boathouse.
There, five generations of the owners of an Adirondack camp

pass a copy of the Declaration from person to person around a table,
taking turns reading aloud   *When in the course*   a designated passage,
it becomes necessary for one people   and hand it to the next.

A fifth generation   *these truths to be self-evident*   toddles, unsteadily,
about the floor   *all men are created equal*   with her sippy cup.
Massive logs braced with tree limbs   *evinces a design to reduce them*

under absolute Despotism   hold up the roof.   *The history
of the present King*   Its overhang and the railings   *is a history
of repeated injuries*   frame the forest undulating around a lake

pocked with islands.   *obstructing the Laws for Naturalization
of Foreigners*   Wind crinkles a patch of water. A wooden Chris Craft
motors by setting the water   *plundered our seas,*   to sloshing

harder   *destroyed the lives of our people*   under the boathouse.
Across the lake, through a dip in the trees, two ridges fade
circumstances of Cruelty & Perfidy scarcely paralleled   into the mist.

In the foreground, the long arm of a pine entreats. A hemlock's limbs
dangle down   *deaf to the voice of justice*   and the occupants
of this landscape   *these United Colonies, are and of Right ought to be*

Free and Independent   pass the past and who we are, and how we came
to be, into the present, Jefferson's language   *we mutually pledge to each other*
our Lives   marrying with theirs, his words inhaled into their bodies.

Then, 56 names, each signer, are tolled, one by one, around the table,
many signing away their lives with that stroke of the pen.
Button Gwinnett. Lyman Hall. George Walton. William Hooper. Joseph. . . .

The names linger in the air.   We are here.

TAPPING SURVIVAL

Listen to my feet and I'll tell you the story of my life.
—JOHN "BUBBLES" SUBLETT

This is what you'll need. Tap shoes.
A hardwood floor, unvarnished, unwaxed.
Maple and oak are least likely
to splinter. And air, plenty of air. It's the air
under the floor that makes the stage a drum
to carry a message the way drums did back home

when the deep bass of your heel
strikes the ground, followed by the little clip
of your toe, the side of your foot sounding
like it's clearing its throat, or whispering,
making a sneaky slide before
the ball of your foot snares the melody.

And a screwdriver, small, to loosen the taps,
so the sound is not so crisp.
Forget the smiles.
This is not the time for smiles.
And keep your arms out of it.
This is not show tap. It's the story.

Play it for keeps. For real. This means
no hips. Legs should hang from the hips

as from a skeleton, or a man
at the end of a rope,
the feet swinging
from loose ankles, the better

to let the spirit out. See
how light the body is unburdened
by the soul, how it skims the floor
like a dragonfly searching
for its beat, for the voice
buried within the beat, for the spot

on the drum that gives that dead-type
tom-tom sound. And *Fuh-DAP!* Hit it!
Eyes front, so no one suspects.
Lay down your iron! Talk.
Show *boom-dah-dee-boom* nothing
DIGgitey-boom above the hips! This

is about time, *tickety-bloo-ka-SHUCK*,
passing, and not passing. This is about
staying alive, you "spittin' out the verbs,"
tapping to be heard, tapping
on the lid of the earth, pretending
shaff-da-boom you're whistling Dixie.

THE GWB IN THE RAIN

Early April. Ice cold and drained of color
as fingertips cut off from oxygen.
Heading south on the Henry Hudson

the road bends, and through the mist
and skeletal tangle of tree trunks and branches
a bridge appears, erased

and returned by the windshield wipers.
Suspenders thin as harp strings
hike the horizontal span to paired catenaries

so much the color of the day they look
drawn in pencil on the sky, their swooping volume
(four feet in diameter and made of enough

miles of wire to crank us halfway
to the moon) reading like paper pouring
through a watercolor, like the silence in music.

Water, cliffs, sky, birds flicker in the X's and V's
of its unsheathed piers and towers, the girders
soaring up through space singing

———

with the economy of a poem
held captive by its form, claiming
no more of the heavens and earth

than necessary to do its job. Looked at
from outside the car, the landscape's palette
of grays and browns, and our black umbrella,

frame the steel bridge drifting
into clouds draped like angel hair
over the leafless trees feathering the Palisades.

To anyone on the New Jersey side
Manhattan must look the same, the bridge's
thrust anchoring into clouds

masking the 179th Street anchorage, a picture
of just how ghostly the connection
between Manhattan and America is.

To the figures on barges plying the river,
and on the restored brigantine materializing
under power from the white breath of the Hudson's

mouth, who see the bridge more nearly dead on,
the toy cars and trucks skimming its motion
east and west must seem to drive

FRIDAY, THE 13TH

From another time zone, *ping*, through the ether, my daughter
makes contact. "If you've heard the news, we're safe." News?
Safe? I'm on West 14th Street, New York City, a squiggle of paint
out of Bruegel, rush hour rushing around me in its rush-hour tempo.
I climb into a cab to go home, and climb into the news.
Paris! Under attack! 352 wounded. 99 critically. Body count 129
and rising. ISIS! Broadcasters are in their nonstop coverage voice.
Hollande declares it is an act of war! Outside, we glide by the gleaming,
well-lit targets of Madison Avenue, laden with prayers to mammon.
I lean over the front seat the better to hear.
"My daughter is there! My daughter!" I tell the driver.
He turns up the volume. Drives faster, as if that would help.
The shopwindows blur. Inside, I'm checking my phone for maps,
looking for the red teardrops marking the attack sites.
Check the address of my daughter's hotel. Dear god, it's

in the Marais! It's near the concert hall! One of the restaurants!
The radio says the rampage began about 9:30 p.m.
Nine-thirty? That's when her son, our grandson, would be
settling down in a youth hostel near the Île de la Cité,
his first night alone in Paris, an American suburban kid
on his first night alone in a city anywhere.
She would have been boarding the train for Beaune,
but I know she didn't. I know she reached her son.
There is that "we" in the email. Did she miss the train?

Did she hear the gunshots, the sirens, before the train left?
I can see her dropping everything, running through the dark,
running hard, running south down the rue Amelot,
right on the rue du Chemin Vert, running and running,
left onto the Boulevard Beaumarchais, to rue Saint-Antoine,
legs pumping, heart pounding, the fear not for her life,
not of where the next bullets might come from,
but fear for her son. No other thought. No other.
All over Paris people are running, running with one thought,
to find their loved ones. All over the world, we run beside them.
What some of them find will rip open the heavens.

WATERCOLORS WITH
SOUND EFFECTS

The clouds have been streaked all day with sky,
the sun falling in odd slivers on the bluff,
in glittering shards on the water, spotlighting
sails crossing it, heightening, for long minutes,
the yellow clumps of daylilies, splayed
against the unlit marsh behind them.

Near seven o'clock the clouds opened and sunlight
spread over the seascape like the fourth movement
of Sibelius's First. Birds burst into their languages,
the sun unbottling all they needed to air
to settle tribal scores, before nestling into sleep.
Their notes kept time to their wingbeats—the gulls'

slow guttural squawk and glide, the swallows'
busy tittering, the goldfinches' throat-stopping
rollercoaster dives and tweeting ascents.
The egret with its hesitant, cautious jerk
makes not a sound tiptoeing about the inlet
with the conviction of a spy. Rabbits

perform their bedtime rituals, oblivious,
licking their paws, scrubbing their faces,
nibbling the bugs out of their haunches.

The osprey, out of sorts all day with its mate,
does not budge from its sulk, or its refuge
atop the mast of a Laser tied up at the dock,

both far and near enough to keep an eye on the nest
without walking out on his mate completely.
The sky begins emptying its color into the next
time zone. The pond fills like a mirror
doubling the wetlands, pulling the sky and clouds
to its surface so perfectly one can't tell clouds

from sandbars, birds flying over it
from their reflection. Lights coming on
across the pond mingle with fireflies.
Beyond, a sloop heads into the harbor
under power, crossing the still air, unheard,
its single sail set for stability.

LISTENING TO THE RADIO

We sit opposite each other in easy chairs, reading,
our feet touching on the hassock. From Public Radio's
wallpaper of music, a story emerges.
We look up. Our eyes lock. We watch the story
play in the other's eyes, see each word
come at the same time.

Night swallows the walls. The story ends.
We don't move. Floor lamps next to our chairs
cast us in separate spheres of light. Is this
how one of us will die? Our eyes coupled?
How the one who lives on will couple
only with death, the way the prey and the wolf

look, for a long moment, in each other's eyes,
acknowledging the story, acknowledging
the minute the prey turns and runs,
the compact between them changes?
We return to our books, floating in the lamplight
like celestial bodies, a Bach partita supplying the ether.

IN BED WITH AN OLD MAN

It's a double bed. Also known as a full. They measure 54" x 75".
You may not be familiar with them.
They predate Queens, which predated Kings,
and were themselves an upgrade of twin beds
for married couples, as seen in 1930s movies.
They were thought to be healthier for you,
and also less likely to give moviegoers ideas.
Back when the old man was a young man,
he brought me to spend the summer with his mother.
My bags were put down in the guest room,
the one with twin beds. What a row that caused.
"Mama! We are married! We want to be in the same bed."
"Sonny! That is not healthy! You won't get your proper rest."
(I should hope not.) He won, but the war wasn't over.
Every morning at breakfast she would look grim, and say,
"Sonny, you don't look like you are getting your proper rest."
What we were getting was entirely proper
now that we were married. And we remained healthy.
Bear in mind, I'm his age-appropriate woman, or close enough
to know the names of the TV shows he watched as a kid,
and also to have danced to Lester Lanin, and now
to have a tummy fat enough to make him worry
it's a disease. I tell him the disease is called
old age. He doesn't believe me.
We do not use Viagra. Make of that what you will.

As we shut down our laptops, perhaps the new safe sex,
and go into a cuddle, naked as the day we were born—
and the only way to sleep in a double bed
when the old man is 6'5" and 195 lbs.—his skin
is still as soft as the day we first coupled.
We turn out the lights, and the rest, oh, the rest,
you with your eye to the keyhole, it is so sweet.

NOTES

"Portrait of My Husband Reading Henry James" is intended to reflect the diction and rhythms of James. He considered "summer afternoon" to be the two most beautiful words in the English language. In the opening of *Portrait of a Lady* he uses the expression "the perfect middle of a splendid summer afternoon." For the purposes of the poem, I substituted the word "rainy" for "splendid."

The title "LINES composed at Beaufort, South Carolina, a few miles above Parris Island" and the opening lines evoke Wordsworth's Tintern Abbey. Wordsworth has a sister in his poem. I have a brother. While the settings of both are away from the "big cities," Wordsworth finds comfort and love in his. My setting offers no comfort, only the "still sad music of humanity," and the narrator hunts through past and present for signs of love's salvation.

The poem's "Miss Judith" refers to the Judith of the apocryphal Book of Judith. She was a "young widow of three years and four months," and the "fairest and purist," who saved her people from slaughter by beheading the invading general, Holofernes. It is the subject of many paintings and sculptures.

"Tabby" is a concrete used in the houses in Beaufort. It is a mixture of oyster shells, lime, sand, and water.

The "A" recalls Hawthorne's Hester Prynne.

"Jacob and Esau with Sister" is straight from the Bible, but the brothers are archetypical figures who appear in many families down to the present.

The inspiration for "Tapping Survival" comes from watching Savion Glover, called the world's greatest tap dancer, since he was twelve years old. Tapping can tell a story as the drums did in Africa. Glover has been using tap, until recently, to tell the story of African Americans in this country to keep the history alive. This is also America's story. The early tappers each had a unique style. Glover incorporates some of their steps as a remembrance. The calling of the rhythms in the last part of the poem is from him. It is the way he tells himself and his dancers where he wants the beat to fall. The quotation "spittin' out the verbs" is directly from him.

John "Bubbles" Sublett, quoted in the epigraph, was one of the early tappers.